17
mp
21
25
f
29

Clowns

F.H. Losey
arr. Jeff Schaum

Andantino ♩= 112 - 120

17
mf
21
f
25
poco a poco cresc.
ff
29

Trapeze Artistry

Gaston Lyle
arr. Jeff Schaum

24
mp
cresc.
30
f
rit.
a tempo
36
mf
f
42
poco rit.

Entry of the Gladiators

Julius Fucik
arr. Jeff Schaum

20
24
29
simile
33

Burr's Triumphal March

R. Alexander
arr. Jeff Schaum

Allegro vivo ♩ = 160 - 176